# Haunted Inns
# of Cornwall

### Robert Hesketh

Bossiney Books

## Author's acknowledgements

This book was made possible by the active co-operation of landlords, land-ladies and inn staff who generously shared their supernatural experiences with me and were so helpful in showing me their haunted inns and in facilitating the photographs. Thanks also to my wife, Adrienne, who accompanied me on my investigations and ably assisted with interviewing and with her own insights into the unseen worlds around us.

*The cover photo is of the Eliot Arms at Tregadillet, and the title page shows Jamaica Inn*

First published 2018 by
Bossiney Books Ltd, 67 West Busk Lane, Otley, LS21 3LY
www.bossineybooks.com
ISBN 978-1-906474-59-1

Photographs by the author, www.roberthesketh.co.uk
Printed in Great Britain by R Booth Ltd, Penryn, Cornwall

## Admiral Benbow, Chapel Street, Penzance

The Admiral Benbow is a listed 18th century building named after Admiral John Benbow, who died of chain-shot wounds sustained fighting the French in the West Indies in 1702. On the roof is the figure of a smuggler – a reminder that the inn was reputedly headquarters of a smuggling gang called the Benbow Brandy Men. Within are souvenirs from *Treasure Island*, by Robert Louis Stevenson, the opening chapters of which novel are set at the 'Admiral Benbow', located in 'Black Cove'.

It is easy to imagine the Captain, Blind Pew and Long John Silver dropping in for a rum or three. Probably both the setting and the inn were the product of Stevenson's fertile imagination, ignited by places he visited – including Penzance for a fortnight in August 1877 – although some authorities claim a Bristol pub, the Llandoger Trow, was his inspiration.

Recognized by CAMRA for its outstanding historic importance, the Admiral Benbow is packed to the rafters with fascinating maritime artefacts. These include ship's figureheads, carvings and timbers, model ships, lanterns, ropes, a diver's helmet, a mariner's telescope and much, much more besides. This remarkable

*The figurehead from HMS Gunvor*

maritime collection is the legacy of Cornish marine salvor, Roland Marsh, who renovated the Admiral Benbow in the 1960s and whose most noted finds were from HMS *Colossus*, a 74-gun Royal Navy ship wrecked off the Scilly Isles in 1798.

My wife, Adrienne, who has accompanied me on all my visits for this book, believes that historic artefacts can bring spiritual presences with them from outside, especially when those artefacts are associated with powerful emotional experiences. She had a strong impression of the sea and a sense of drowning and darkness as we explored both floors of this extraordinary inn, filled as they are with treasures recovered from shipwrecks. Possibly it is these presences which members of staff have encountered in various ways.

Judy Roger has worked for a long time at the Admiral Benbow and gradually become used to its aura, confident nothing will harm her. However, some of her experiences have been disconcerting.

'When I walk past the ship's figurehead from HMS *Gunvor* by the stairs I feel she's watching me, even though her eyes are opaque,' Judy said. '... Sometimes I have a feeling of a presence I can't

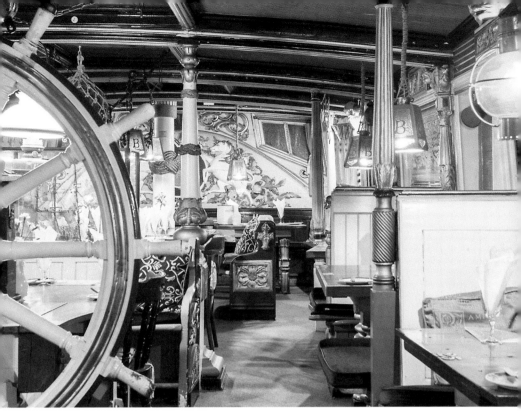

explain. Once, I was in the restaurant on my own, when the hairs on my head and the back of my neck stood up on end and I felt really cold. I thought "I don't like this at all," you know how it is, your imagination runs riot – and then suddenly a cushion fell forward and there was no way it could have moved without someone or something pushing it, it was too heavy…'

Barman Matt Howells also recalled an encounter with an unseen guest: 'I had been cleaning in the function room. When I returned, I noticed the door moving of its own accord. At first, it moved just a few inches – then it swung right open. What freaked me out is that this is a *self-closing* door and you have to use quite a bit of force to open it.'

Trish McGregor, the landlady at the Admiral Benbow, had a similar and very unnerving experience: 'The empty chair by the fire started moving and creaking, as though someone was sitting on it and wriggling around. You know how it is when you're so scared you can't move? Well, I was *that scared*.'

## The Angel Hotel, Coinagehall Street, Helston

Beginning as a town house for the powerful Godolphin family in the 16th century, the Angel Hotel has had a long and varied history at the centre of Helston life. In the 1690s it became an inn, but was also used as an excise house and a temporary jail for smugglers – one of whom escaped by getting his jailers drunk. In 1756, it was described as a 'house of great business and good accommodations with a large cock-pit built after one of the best models.'

Helston gained a reputation as a hard-drinking town. John and Charles Wesley described it as 'a storm centre' and found it long resistant to the religious revival they ignited more easily in less bibulous places. In Victorian times, the Angel settled into a more respectable role as Helston's main coaching and posting house, as well as being a Masonic centre and an Inland Revenue office.

However, the most dramatic and tragic incident in the Angel's long history occurred in 1975. After a furious argument the landlord, Valentine Ohlenschlager, ordered one of his staff – who had been drinking heavily – to bed. Both had served in the Navy and Captain Ohlenschlager considered it was case closed, until the man reappeared 'looking drunk and wild' and waving an automatic pistol. Without warning, he fired eight or nine shots around the crowded bar. Ohlenschlager bravely moved forward to protect the barmaids and was struck by five bullets. He died on the way to hospital and two customers were also wounded. The gunman was subsequently convicted of manslaughter.

'When the paranormal group visited, they stayed for two days and reported three spirits around the well in the bar,' said barman Zach Collins. 'They also found several other spirits, and identified some by name, including Nellie, a young girl who hung herself from the banister in the Georgian ballroom. Some guests have said they've seen Nellie. Others claimed they heard her walking along the landing and unexplained voices at night.

'Personally, I haven't experienced anything definitely supernatural,' continued Zach, who's lived and worked at the Angel for six years. 'Perhaps I've been here so long the spirits have got used to me.'

## Bucket of Blood, Phillack

Legend has it the Bucket of Blood, a listed building dating from at least the 18th century, was a haven for smugglers.

One morning, the landlord went to his deep well to draw water – and was aghast to draw up a bucket of blood. A mutilated body was discovered at the bottom of the well, reputedly that of a revenue officer who had been investigating contraband activity in the area.

Not surprisingly, there have been several reports of supernatural activity at the inn. These range from ghostly figures crossing the road outside to creaking floorboards.

*Opposite: The Georgian ballroom at the Angel Hotel*

## The Bush Inn, Morwenstow

'As a sceptic, I was up there with the best of them,' said Colin Fletcher, who took over at the historic Bush Inn three years ago with his wife and son. 'Rather naively, I thought that if I couldn't see it or touch it, nothing was real. But not long after we arrived my views started to change…

'Most weeks something or other happened which I couldn't necessarily explain. I was sure I'd heard footsteps upstairs and furniture being moved around when I knew full well I was alone, but my first sighting occurred one evening when I was at the bar. I saw a lady in an antique dress beckoning me to come over to her.

It was a quiet evening and I knew there hadn't been anyone in her seat previously. Well, I went over… and there was no one there.

'One morning I was on my own filling the fridges when I had a sense there was someone behind me. I turned round to see a different lady sitting on a stool watching me. She was in her fifties, had curly hair and was wearing modern clothes. Suddenly, she was no longer there.

'I've had similar encounters in the corridor. Again, these people are often, though not always, dressed in modern or fairly modern clothing. My most memorable encounter with someone in traditional dress – and the most dramatic of the sightings I've had here – was when I saw a man in a tricorn hat and a black cloak walk across the conservatory and out through the window. It was like something out of *Poldark*. Strangely, the conservatory is by far the newest part of this ancient building. It was only built a few years ago, though there might well have been some earlier structure there.

'None of these experiences has unnerved me, though there was a chap who worked here before our time who never wanted to be on his own at the Bush again after some experience he'd had here late at night. Strange, isn't it?'

## Crown Inn, St Ewe

St Ewe's Crown Inn is tucked away among the green hills between St Austell and Mevagissey. According to a plaque on the wall of the bar, it was built in 1601 by the Rev. Hugh Atwill and was originally a rectory, with parts of the adjoining property used as poor houses. It's not clear exactly when it became an inn, but the list of landlords and ladies goes back to 1841.

'It seems that funny things happen here January or February time,' said landlord Ernie Heather. 'It's nothing unusual for a glass of wine to slide off Table One for no reason whatsoever.

'The former landlord died on Burns Night in 2013,' he continued. 'A year later, they had a family reunion. There was a full glass of wine on Table Ten. It came up off the table, upset and dropped, but the daughter caught it before it smashed on the table. A mate of mine saw it and was gobsmacked.'

Ernie showed us two mysterious digital images taken at Table Ten on different nights by different people. The first print was a surprise to the photographer. He had intended to take a close up image of the food on the table. Everything is blurred and out of focus, with strange S-shaped patterns of light.

The second print was not only a surprise, but a shock too. It shows two men and a boy seated at a table. Although the people in the photograph didn't feel anything was strange or amiss when the image was taken, they discovered two wraith-like forms hovering over them in the print. The smaller of the two forms resembles a dog's head, whilst the larger looks like the upper body and head of a man. The eye sockets and the skull are particularly prominent and the shape of the shoulders distinct.

Now, the younger of the two men refuses to go near Table Ten. Stranger still, the Newfoundland Labrador cross dog kept by Ernie's partner – an animal not easily spooked – avoids Table Ten too.

## Crow's Nest Inn, Darite

The 17th century Crow's Nest Inn in Bodmin Moor's Caradon mining district has served several purposes over the years. It's a substantial building and the oldest recorded in the village; it was once a mine captain's house and the pay office for local miners, who were summoned by the bell which stands on the outside wall. Miners were partly paid in Crow's Nest tokens, which could be exchanged for goods and ale at the office. Bought by St Austell Brewery in 1905, it was known as the Sun Inn until 1985.

CROWS NEST INN CROWS NEST IN

'I'd like to tell you I've heard mysterious footsteps or presences passing the window, but I haven't and I haven't had any cold shivers either,' said tenant Jenny Heard, who met us in the bar. As we were talking, one of the tankards hanging from a hook over the bar began to swing of its own accord. This did not entirely surprise Jenny, who once saw a full pint of beer swept sideways off the bar to land without a breath of wind or any human intervention.

'It was my pint too,' said Jenny with feeling. 'It went with quite a *whoosh* and landed upright on the floor tiles. Fortunately, the glass was intact, so I just told him off – I think he's the former landlord who died behind the bar – and filled my glass up again. Another time, I saw a water jug fly off the bar shelf… that was witnessed by three other people.'

'Behind the bar there's a container for straws and serviettes,' added Martin McConn, who shares the tenancy with Jenny. 'It's normally wedged behind the till. Well, I was standing behind the bar when I saw it shoot off and land in the bottle bin with such force as though someone had picked it up and thrown it down. It

12

made a hell of a racket, but nothing was broken, not even the bottles. All the people at the bar jumped when they heard it! Oddly, none of the straws or serviettes were out of place either.'

We glanced at the pub clock which stands above the massive fireplace. It showed closing time was nigh, but as it always runs ten minutes fast and is reputed to re-set itself or even jump off the wall if tampered with, there appeared to be just time for another one. I grasped my pint firmly.

## Eliot Arms, Tregadillet

The Eliot Arms lies on the old coaching route two miles west of Launceston and is thought to have served as an inn since the 17th century. For many years it was known as the Square & Compass, a clue to its being a meeting place for the Freemasons. During the 18th and early 19th centuries several leading Masons were French officer prisoners billeted in the Launceston area. However, it is the spirit of a young girl who is most often reported at the inn.

'Three people have told me they've seen her sitting on the settle in the bar holding a rag doll,' said landlord Chris Hume. 'When a photo was taken of a man playing darts on his own in the neighbouring room, she appeared on the print.'

'I've never actually seen anything strange, but I often have a feeling of being watched, especially in the kitchen and the passage at the back,' continued Jo Andrew, who's worked at the Eliot Arms for over twenty years. 'I have heard some strange things too. Once, when I was working in the kitchen, I heard singing, a girl's voice. I was working with a colleague, so I asked her what she was singing. She said she wasn't – she thought it was me singing.

'Another time I was in the bar once with my husband on a quiet winter's evening, when we heard heavy footsteps on the floor above. I asked the barman if we had any residents in the letting rooms. He looked surprised and said "No, but there must be someone up there." So, thinking it might be an intruder, he went upstairs and looked in the beds, the wardrobes, everywhere, but could find nobody.

'Other strange things happen upstairs. The kettle switches itself on and off, the toilet flushes when there's nobody there. Then things just disappear for no reason. We blame the old landlord who died a number of years ago. Sometimes we find the missing objects in the weirdest places.'

## Jamaica Inn

A few miles further west along the A30 lies the Jamaica Inn, which is widely known through Daphne du Maurier's melodramatic smuggling novel *Jamaica Inn*. First published in 1936, du Maurier's story has been dramatized several times for television and for the cinema, most famously by Alfred Hitchcock in 1939, when Charles Laughton and Maureen O'Hara took the lead roles.

Jamaica Inn dates from the late 18th century, when smuggling (or 'The Free Trade' as its practitioners preferred to call it) was at its height in Cornwall. It is reputed to be haunted by a variety of spirits. We spoke to two of the staff about their own experiences.

'There are definitely spiritual presences here,' said Julia Lawrence, who's worked in a variety of roles over the past twenty years. 'We host a lot of events, paranormal investigations and ghost hunts. Some groups use the inn regularly, with people staying overnight. They get a lot of success using Ouija boards.

'When I started here, I didn't feel comfortable at all in some parts, especially the museum and the rooms above the bar… I felt that people were watching me all the time. There were some nights when I locked up I was so frightened I'd run from room to room. It's when it first happens to you that you feel shocked and awed, but you get used to it with time, you live with it, it becomes the norm, like part of the family walking through.'

Barman Ian Chambers has worked at the Jamaica Inn for nine years: 'There's something about the Jamaica Inn which drags some people in. It *chooses you*, as though it knows who it likes and who it wants to stay. We've had some brilliant staff who've left soon after they came, but it seems like others are *wanted*.

'I'd heard of the Jamaica Inn's reputation, but was a bit sceptical when I first started working here, as I'd never had any supernatural experiences before. After I'd been here a couple of weeks there was one of our regular ghost hunts with Ouija boards. No one else was in the bar area where I was. Suddenly, I got a very stern prodding sensation in my side, just above my ribs. There was no mistaking it. I shot up, expecting to see someone – but there was no one there.

'Well, that was quite an eye opener… The first few weeks here were a bit tense, especially as it was my job to lock up at night. I was all alone and had the creepy sensation that someone was watching me, especially in the museum. A lot of people have an oppressive feeling in there.

'A frequent and very freaky occurrence is glasses, which don't just drop off the shelves, but land some distance away on the other side of the bar. It's not just vibrations that do that, the glasses are somehow *pushed*. Similarly, the jugs which hang on hooks above the bar tend to swing, even when there's no one there to cause it.'

## King's Head, Altarnun

'Weird things happen here for no apparent reason. You can explain most of them away, but…. well, let me tell you about some of them,' said Mandy Bettison, landlady of the 18th century King's Head at Altarnun on the northern edge of Bodmin Moor.

'My Aunty Judy, who ran the King's Head for many years, often saw a little girl in a white dress – though I've never seen her, which is really annoying. Once, Judy woke to find her sitting at the foot of her bed. A customer also saw the child late one evening, mistaking her blonde hair for my aunt's. I told him he was mistaken, as Judy had gone to bed ages before. This frightened him. He told me he was shaking like a leaf and wasn't right for days afterwards.

'Something strange always happens after the paranormal group come here to investigate. Last time they stayed overnight and the fire alarm went off twice in the night, both times for no reason. I wasn't best pleased by that, nor by the time all the bottles suddenly shot off the shelf in the dining room and exploded on the floor – though the customers thought this was hilarious!

'Another time, I found the till full of water and had to dry the bank notes in the carvery before I could count my takings. We've had the cooker turn itself on and off, once melting the barmaid's car keys.

'The paranormal group invited me to join them once. A lady said she had contacted the daughter of a former landlord and began asking her all these questions using a crystal on a string, like a pendulum. She told the spirit to swing her pendulum one way for "yes" and the other way for "no". The lady was doing nothing more than holding the pendulum at the end of her arm, but it spun around like crazy and the lady started to cry. It was really creepy… and the lady was totally exhausted at the end of it all.

'Strange things happen upstairs as well. We had a lady staying in Room 3 who was woken by six sharp taps on the window. She checked to see if it was the wind that caused the noise, but it wasn't.

'A fisherman who stays here regularly said he had someone outside his door playing with the handle all night, but that didn't bother him. We had a long term resident staying in the same room, Room 2, who often saw a man in a black cape staring out of the window, though he never saw his face as he always had his back turned.

'None of these things seem to put people off coming to the King's Arms,' concluded Mandy as she pulled us pints in the bar, 'rather it draws them. The paranormal people, who've often been, tell me there are only good spirits left here at the King's Head.'

## Miner's Arms, Mithian

The Miner's Arms in Mithian near St Agnes is a listed historic building. Altered and added to several times, it is said to have served several functions from court house to brothel over the past four centuries.

'When we first moved in ten years ago they [the resident ghosts] were quite excited, but we barely hear from them now,' said landlady Anouska House. 'We've been here so long they've got used to us, but they used to make loads of noise, dragging stools and moving cutlery and table numbers about.

'They usually start messing around at the end of summer if the visitors have annoyed them. Sometimes they pick on people. The last landlord's daughter was always the centre of attention. She was hit in the back by a clock that flew off the wall, and again with a blunt knife.

'Her mother always kept her purse in the same place, so it was handy for paying visiting tradesmen, but it was often moved. In the end, this lady lost her temper and shouted at them *Bloody well put it back!* … and they did. That was the only time she's had proper communication with them.

'Please promise me you won't speak to the ghosts. I have to live with them! If people try to talk to them there's always a problem. Once, we allowed a medium and his friends to film their meal in the Chapel Room. I told him not to speak to the ghosts, but he did anyway. It freaked me right out. They drained the battery of his dicataphone, which the medium had hidden away in the cupboard without my knowledge. They drained the two full batteries on his video recorder as well and turned it off too. I told him all this had happened because they didn't want you to talk to them.

'Well, the next morning I went to the cupboard to get my cleaning stuff as usual. I always say "Good Morning" to them… but that morning it felt really awful. Wherever I went it felt like there was someone stood over my back… That is the worst they've ever been, touch wood. It's nice that we work together now and not in opposition. We're accepted.'

*The Chapel Room in the Miner's Arms at Mithian*

## New Inn, Goonhavern

Goonhavern's New Inn was refurbished in 2013, but period photographs in the bar show it is much older than it looks now. It has been an inn since 1871, though it is thought to be much older than that according to Senior Supervisor, Kelly Johnson.

Kelly went on to tell us of a woman who passed away in one of the upstairs rooms. Whether she died by her own hand or not is uncertain, but after this sad event the room was walled off and can only be accessed by a small hatch.

'We keep our Christmas decorations there, but I'm not brave enough to go up,' admitted Kelly. 'She was called Annie and people say they have seen her spirit in the pool room, below what was her bedroom.'

Another presence which has been reported is that of a former customer, a regular at the inn, called Derek. Although he passed away some ten years ago, it seems he still is a regular and is seen in his favourite corner of the New Inn.

'There are certainly some presences here, but it's not scary,' continued Kelly. 'Although I've stayed here at night when it was pitch black there was nothing to make you feel uneasy… I've seen people walk past me to the bar, but when I've gone down to serve them there was nobody there and I'm sure it wasn't people outside walking past the windows.'

## Old Albion Inn, Crantock

'I did feel a bit uncomfortable when we first arrived at the Old Albion,' said landlady Evelyn Burdett, 'but I think that was because it had been neglected and was cold and damp. It's fine now we've made it a living place again.

'There was a family living next door in Lychgate Cottage, which we now rent out to visitors, who used to experience strange things from a friendly but mischievous entity. They identified her as Mrs Beecham, a former resident. She frequented her lounge… I guess because she could enjoy the heat from our bar fire that shares the same wall and chimney.

'Some time ago, when we were having the cottage renovated, I took some visitors in to show them around. My husband had left the front door open. For some reason, I had the door keys in my hand. When we came to leave, the front door was locked. Well, I had to unlock it to let us out. I asked Harry – my husband – why he was playing silly buggers with us. "What do you mean?" he said indignantly.

'"Did you lock the door on us?" I demanded.

'"Of course not – you've got the keys!" he retorted.

Harry later had a similar experience. He'd been working in the cottage all day and left the doors open, but when he came to leave he found himself locked in and had to climb out through the window.

'We keep a digital radio upstairs in the cottage which turns itself on,' continued Evelyn. 'Several times I've gone in to find the radio on at full blast, so I took the precaution of disconnecting it from the mains. However, I warn visitors that it may turn itself on randomly…

'The cottage always feels friendly, if that makes sense, but it seems when you start disturbing the place things happen. That's when she – Mrs Beecham I mean – comes out to play.'

*Lychgate Cottage, beside the Old Albion Inn, home of 'Mrs Beecham'*

## Ye Olde Malthouse, Tintagel

'I'm a total sceptic, but try to keep open minded,' said Rafael Krasnodebski, landlord of Ye Olde Malthouse, who came to Tintagel with his family after many years working abroad. 'Our house in Warsaw had a sinister presence you could really feel, but then Warsaw is a city with a tragic past. The place had been built and owned by the Head of the KGB in Poland. He was Jewish, fell victim to the purge of Jewish officials in 1968-69 and fled to New York. People talk about the hairs on the back of your neck standing on end – well mine did, especially in the cellars of that house. Happily, we never get that feeling here at the Malthouse. If there is something here, it isn't scary.

'The two year old son of a neighbour told us there was a man sleeping on the settle in the snug, the room next to the bar. The little boy didn't want to go back there in case he woke the man… he was really *pulling* his parents out of the snug. When we went to look, nobody was there. Whether this is the imagination of a child or not I don't know, but our son – then nine years old – told us

*Bar stools at Ye Olde Malthouse were moved into the snug one night, despite the door being locked*

he'd seen a man who calls himself "Peter" in the same room. Again we checked – and nobody was there.

'The automatic hand dryers in the toilets have infra-red sensors and start off by themselves, often in the middle of the night. It's probably just a breath of wind or a vibration that does it, but this spooks many of the guests, especially if they've heard of the inn's haunted reputation.'

More mysteriously, stools that are always kept in the bar were moved into the snug one night despite the intervening door being locked. 'When I locked up at night everything was where it should have been,' said Barbara, Rafael's wife, 'but in the morning the stools had moved. I asked the other staff if they'd moved the stools, but they hadn't and were as puzzled as I was. I have no idea how they got there.'

The upper rooms of Ye Olde Malthouse are also haunted, according to Becky Thacker, who has worked at the inn for seven years. 'It's quite creepy sometimes. I always feel cold in Room 4. It gives me goose bumps, but I always say "Hello" to him when I make the beds. This settles him down. I believe he's a friendly presence and once owned the place. He's just there keeping an eye on things.'

## Polgooth Inn

Ruined engine houses and spoil heaps abound in Cornwall, stark reminders of a once vital, but now vanished industry and the hard and dangerous lives of Cornish miners. Mining was integral to many Cornish communities, not least Polgooth near St Austell. By the 18th century, the village was celebrated as 'the greatest tin mine in the world' and employed over 1000 people. The Polgooth Inn was used as a count house, where the miners were paid. This is said to have nearly caused a revolt by miners' wives, outraged at their husbands squandering their wages on drink before returning home. A law was passed banning the payment of miners at public houses, and a separate count house was recorded in Polgooth in 1791.

Completed in 1828 on the site of the original 17th century inn, the present Polgooth Inn has many reminders of Polgooth's mining history. These include the pub sign, showing a mine engine house, period photographs, an evocative collection of miners'

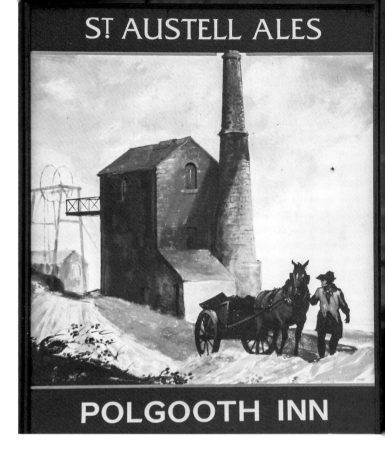

photographic portraits … and supernatural presences.

'I saw the same ghostly figure in the cellar of the Polgooth Inn twice on the same day,' said Darren Heather, recalling the time when he was chef there. 'This was a long time ago, but what I saw made a strong impression on me. He was dressed in black trousers, a black hat and a white shirt and looked like a miner… He didn't frighten me at all, but the experience did shake me up a bit. When I told the then landlady, she said she had seen the same figure herself.

Darren now runs the 16th century inn Kings Arms at Tregony a few miles westward, which is also said to be haunted. His colleague, Wendy Eade, is still at the Polgooth Inn and told us she felt presences there quite regularly: 'There was no nasty feeling,' said Wendy, 'and I didn't feel frightened – but then I live in a haunted cottage in Polgooth.'

## Tinners Arms, Zennor

The Tinners Arms is a listed historic building opposite Zennor church on the remote and rocky coast of West Penwith. Portraits of former customers drawn in 1945 stand by the window near the fireplace. One is of a former landlord, another of a man who brought rabbits to the pub. However, it is not they, but two old ladies who are said to haunt this area, according to manager John Levine. The ghost of a miner stands in the doorway, watching the clientele and another spirit haunts the bay window of the white house next door, which is let to visitors.

We can only guess what the resident spirits thought when author D H Lawrence and his German wife Frieda paid a short and turbulent visit during the First World War. It was a time of widespread anti-German sentiment, prompting the royal family to change their name to Windsor from Saxe-Coburg and Gotha.

Speaking out against the war did not endear Lawrence and

Frieda to local people, who mistook the bearded author and his Scottish friend Cecil Gray's renderings of Gaelic songs for German lyrics. Under suspicion of colluding with the enemy, Lawrence and Frieda were summarily ordered out of Cornwall by the authorities in 1917.

Beside the haunted fireplace in the bar is a splendid stone carving of the Zennor Mermaid, a faithful copy of the original 15th century mermaid carving in the church. Legend has it that Matthew Trewhella, son of the squire and a church chorister, had a fine singing voice. Morveren, a beautiful mermaid, whose own voice was bewitching, heard his song and came to the church to listen. Smitten with love at the purity of his song, she lured him into the sea at Pendour Cove. Neither man nor mermaid was ever seen again, though it is said that their lovely voices, joined in

*The haunted fireplace, with the mermaid to its right*

*Carving of a Cornish miner by the entrance to the Tinner's Arms, Zennor*

harmony, can be heard on warm summer evenings. Had Matthew read Homer's *Odyssey* he would have recognized the danger of Morveren's siren voice...

On the carving, the Zennor Mermaid's pose is similar to classical depictions of Aphrodite, the goddess of love and the sea. However, the Mermaid does not carry a quince (love apple) as Aphrodite was wont to do, but a comb for her beautiful hair and a mirror – symbol of vanity. The Greek goddess of love was absorbed into the Cornish Christian tradition in medieval times, when a mermaid performed in 'miracle plays' to represent the dual nature of Christ – both God and man – just as mermaids are both fish and human.

Although other Cornish churches, including Altarnun and Breage, have medieval wall paintings of mermaids, St Senara's church in Zennor is the only one with an extant mermaid carving. This is apt as St Senara, from whose name Zennor derives, is said to have arrived by sea from Brittany in a barrel.

The balcony of the Assemby Rooms at the Union Hotel where the news of Trafalgar was first announced, together with a face mask of Nelson (below)

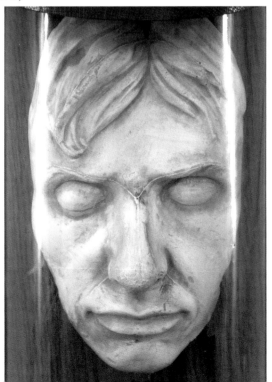

# Union Hotel, Chapel Street, Penzance

The Union Hotel is a handsome Georgian building, particularly noted for the Penzance Assembly Rooms at the rear. It was from the balcony in 1805 that the Mayor of Penzance announced momentous news: the British had won a great naval victory at Trafalgar, but Admiral Horatio Nelson had been killed.

However, it is not the Assembly Rooms that are said to be haunted, but rather the adjoining lounge, as we found when we spoke to manager Howie Williams: 'When Poundland was opening in Penzance,' he began, 'four young women on the staff stayed here at the Union. They were all here in the lounge when they swore they saw something move across the room. They started screaming and ran downstairs. Hours later, they were still so frightened they wouldn't stay alone, but all slept in the same big double bed.

'My only personal experience happened not long after I arrived at the Union. I was a sceptic then. It was my custom to check the rooms on all three floors each evening. Well, I came up to the first floor when I heard music. This is nothing unusual in a hotel and I thought nothing of it. When I climbed to the second floor, the music stopped, but the strange thing was it started again when I got to the top floor. Now, I knew for a fact there was no one staying on the top floor. I could feel the hackles rising on the back of my neck as I ran downstairs. I went straight to the computer to check whether anyone was staying in Room 6, where the music came from. There wasn't. Subsequently, I heard that a woman used to live in that room and entertain guests with her piano. I still find it hard to visit the top floor and get a strange feeling up there. I won't go at night unless someone wants their bags carried up.

'About five or six years ago we had a problem with a guest who'd parked his car over the entrance to the car park, which is also a fire exit. I found out whose car it was and phoned him in his room, Room 19, but he got quite rude when I asked him to drop his car back a few feet.

'I said: "Sir, I don't want to make a big deal of this, but would you mind…." He slammed the phone down on me and then stalked downstairs. We walked out to the car park together and he said: "I

*The Lounge at the Union Hotel*

want to know who runs this hotel, because I'm going to write them a letter, I'm really angry!"

'I said: "There's no point in writing me a letter, I'm right beside you. Don't panic about it. I don't know why you're getting upset, but there'll be a pint of beer waiting for you in the bar for moving your car."

'Well, I thought that was the end of it, but when I came down to breakfast the next morning the same man from Room 19 was there saying he wanted a word with me. He was visibly shaking...

'"Is this place haunted?" he demanded.

'"Yes, it's full of it," I replied.

'"No, I'm being serious!"

'"So am I."

'"Last night, I woke up and there was a guy on the end of my bed reading a book. Seriously... I kept trying to sleep and waking up as this guy got nearer and nearer to me along the bed."

'"That'll teach you to put the phone down on somebody," I thought to myself. I just wouldn't take him seriously, though he was shaking badly and seemed a totally different person from the arrogant so and so of the night before.

'Then the man who was staying next to him in Room 20 piped up and said: "I heard him scream last night, really loud."

'So I turned to our friend from Room 19 and said "Look that wasn't me, I've got my own cottage."

'He said: "Listen, I apologise for my rudeness last night, I was out of order, but that frightened me to death. I'll never stay in your hotel again." He paid his money and he went – he couldn't get out quick enough!

'To this day, I don't know who or what it was sitting on his bed.'

## Victoria Inn, Four Lanes near Redruth

'For me the world is full of presences, which makes it very interesting,' said Susie Willis, a regular customer at the Victoria, an inn which is much older than it now appears after modernisation. 'Cornwall's a particularly spiritual place, maybe because of our pagan past or our Celtic roots.

'I believe there are several different times running concurrently. You don't have to stay in this one all the time, but can move from one to another. Other people can move into our time frame and go again too.

'My partner laughs at me, because he doesn't believe in it, but if you're receptive, you're tuned in to it always, wherever you are. I see presences just like I see you. Sometimes, they talk to me, but I turn off a lot of the time because I don't want to be plagued by them.

'I don't feel there's anything bad here at the Victoria, but there is a lot of activity – more some times than others. One is a spirit who tips me off my stool. He's just being jolly… I presume he was someone who used to drink here. A lot of customers come here with spirits attached to them. One was the grandfather of Belinda, a lady who often visits the Victoria. I later discovered this man had died in a chair over there.

'I see people walking past where we are sitting now, particularly a man in black trousers and a white shirt, but I don't try to communicate with him because he doesn't seem interested in anyone else. There's a lady with a child, and soldiers from the Civil War.

'Spirits are attracted to crossroads and we're right on the junction of four ways here, the old square where the gallows were sited. When I walk down the Piece road from here towards the Countryman Inn and the old mines I can see the miners and hear the stamp engines pounding away. That was a brutal time in some ways and I get the feeling of it.'

I asked Susie whether she thought inns were places that particularly attracted spirits: 'Pubs are eventful places and many have a long history. When you're not drinking you're more preoccupied with your daily worries, but when the alcohol is flowing, people are more open to outside energies because they're not so guarded, so inhibited.'

*The Victoria, at Four Lanes near Redruth*

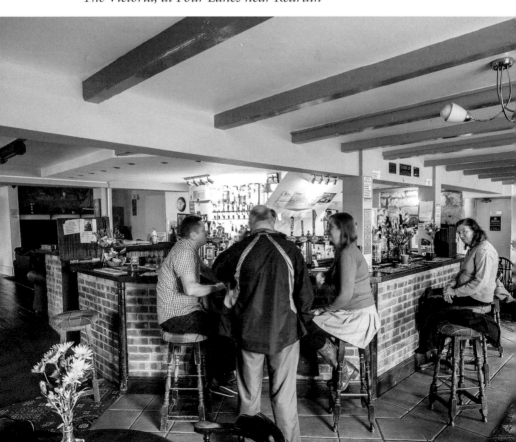

## White Hart Hotel, Hayle

As owner Michael Bowes explained, the White Hart is a Grade II*
listed building and important to Hayle, especially through its
connection with the famous engineering firm, Harvey's of Hayle
– which made the largest steam pumps in the world, used for
both mining and land drainage projects. Harvey's built the White
Hart Hotel for customers from the colonies, who would expect
somewhere to stay in style. The original White Hart Inn is now the
Freemason's Hall at the back of the hotel.

A few years ago, Michael heard that spirits had been interfering
with some of the Masonic ceremonies. He was surprised to meet a
formidable lady in the White Hart bar – 'a real boiling piece, if you
know what I mean' – who cheerfully told him she had succeeded
in moving the troublesome spirits to the White Hart. 'Thank you
very much,' Michael replied ironically.

'People you wouldn't expect to be sensitive or attuned to this
sort of thing have told me they've sensed a lady's hand on their

shoulder,' Michael continued, 'but turning and expecting the waitress trying to attract their attention have found no one there. It's happened to me several times, normally in the bar here or the old restaurant. I know it's a lady's hand because it's soft – you can feel the four fingers and the thumb behind on your back.

'Another thing is we've got a lot of pictures here. Although we try to keep them plumb and square they often move. I don't find these events disconcerting either… but reassuring if anything.'

We asked Bill Gricks, who lives in a flat at the White Hart, about his experiences at the hotel: 'Three things stick in my mind. I was here in the bar one day when Mike saw me do a 360 degree turn. He said to me, "Has someone just tapped you on the shoulder?" I said, "Yes, it was a definite tap," but there wasn't a soul there!

'About a year ago, we had some paranormal researchers come down. Les the barman said they were paying him to stay up to one in the morning, so would I like to have a drink and keep him company? Well, I'm not one to refuse a late night drink… We were sitting in the bar chatting away when suddenly there was a sound of glass breaking. I thought someone had smashed a window, but it was a glass – this hadn't fallen off the bar shelf, it actually flew off and landed in the middle of the room and smashed to pieces.

'I keep my keys and things in a wooden bowl on a table. One day, I opened the front door to my flat when something stopped me in my tracks – there on the floor in the middle of the room was my wooden bowl, with the keys still in it. It hadn't fallen off and tipped over. Naturally, I thought someone must've got in. I searched the place, but there was no one there. When I told Mike the flat's haunted – you know what he said to me? "I'll have to put your rent up because you're co-existing!"

'I'm sort of night watchman here. One night, the alarm went off about half one in the morning. So I checked the place out. I looked to the right, then I looked to the left and there's this white face looking out. It frightened the life out of me! Well, I whipped me torch out and… it was a white balloon someone had left there, dancing around in the draught from the door.'

I asked Bill if he found all this disturbing: 'No, not at all. Mother

*Room 9 at the White Hart Hotel*

was an international medium. You'll probably think I'm as mad as a hatter… but I've been a Pagan since I was sixteen and seen and witnessed so many things it doesn't bother me at all really. It gives me confidence to think there's something on the other side.'

Kaylie Tremeer, who has worked at the White Hart for many years, took us on a tour of the hotel's most haunted rooms. First stop was Room 4, where a guest reported the apparition of a man in the window. The guest woke his wife, who saw the apparition too.

We continued to Room 9, reputedly the hotel's most haunted room: 'I was making the beds in there,' Kaylie said, 'when all the cups and saucers flew off the table and smashed. I made a hasty retreat downstairs and got someone else to clean up!

'I've been here long enough now that I don't mind being in Room 9, but Room 16… we've had some weird incidents there. Well, I don't know if I believe in coincidence, but we've had two people there suffer haemorrhages. The first one survived, the second one didn't.

*Room 16 at the White Hart Hotel*

'Two girls were cleaning up the blood after the first event, when a glass smashed against the wall.

'After the second – in which the guest unfortunately died – one of the girls saw an angry looking man come out of Room 16 and rush towards her before disappearing.'

## More about West Country ghosts from Bossiney Books

*Ghostly encounters*, Peter Underwood
*Ghosts around Bodmin Moor*, Michael Williams
*Ghosts of Cornwall*, Peter Underwood
*Ghosts of Devon*, Peter Underwood
*Ghosts of Dorset*, Peter Underwood
*Ghosts of North Devon*, Peter Underwood
*Ghosts of Somerset*, Peter Underwood
*Haunted Inns of Devon*, Robert Hesketh
*West Country Hauntings*, Peter Underwood